INSIDE THE WORLD OF SPORTS

INSIDE THE WORLD OF SPORTS

AUTO RACING
BASEBALL
BASKETBALL
EXTREME SPORTS
FOOTBALL
GOLF
GYMNASTICS
ICE HOCKEY
LACROSSE
SOCCER
TENNIS
TRACK & FIELD
WRESTLING

INSIDE THE WORLD OF SPORTS

EXTREME SPORTS

by Mason Crest

MASON CREST

Mason Crest
450 Parkway Drive, Suite D
Broomall, Pennsylvania 19008
(866) MCP-BOOK (toll free)

First printing
9 8 7 6 5 4 3 2 1

Title: Extreme sports.
Description: Broomall, Pennsylvania : Mason Crest, [2017] | Series: Inside
 the world of sports | Includes bibliographical references, webography and index.
Identifiers: LCCN 2015046930 (print) | LCCN 2016015611 (ebook) | ISBN
 9781422234594 (Hardback) | ISBN 9781422234556 (Series) | ISBN
 9781422284216 (eBook)
Subjects: LCSH: Extreme sports--History. | ESPN X-Games. | Olympics.
Classification: LCC GV749.7 .E984 2017 (print) | LCC GV749.7 (ebook) | DDC
 796.04/609--dc23
LC record available at https://lccn.loc.gov/2015046930

QR CODES AND LINKS TO THIRD-PARTY CONTENT

You may gain access to certain third-party content ("Third-Party Sites") by scanning and using the QR Codes that appear in this publication (the "QR Codes"). We do not operate or control in any respect any information, products, or services on such Third-Party Sites linked to by us via the QR Codes included in this publication, and we assume no responsibility for any materials you may access using the QR Codes. Your use of the QR Codes may be subject to terms, limitations, or restrictions set forth in the applicable terms of use or otherwise established by the owners of the Third-Party Sites. Our linking to such Third-Party Sites via the QR Codes does not imply an endorsement or sponsorship of such Third-Party Sites, or the information, products, or services offered on or through the Third-Party Sites, nor does it imply an endorsement or sponsorship of this publication by the owners of such Third-Party Sites.

CONTENTS

KEY ICONS TO LOOK FOR:

Words to understand: These words with their easy-to-understand definitions will increase the reader's understanding of the text while building vocabulary skills.

Educational Videos: Readers can view videos by scanning our QR codes, providing them with additional educational content to supplement the text. Examples include news coverage, moments in history, speeches, iconic sports moments and much more!

Text-dependent questions: These questions send the reader back to the text for more careful attention to the evidence presented there.

Research projects: Readers are pointed toward areas of further inquiry connected to each chapter. Suggestions are provided for projects that encourage deeper research and analysis.

In the past 30 years, athletes with a new attitude toward competitive sport and a fearless disregard for their own safety have created action, or extreme, sports. These are counterculture activities like skateboarding, snowboarding and BMX racing that have found mainstream popularity and success.

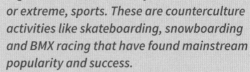

CHAPTER 1

EXTREME SPORTS' GREATEST MOMENTS

Most American sports involve an athlete doing battle against another athlete, either individually or as part of a team. What makes extreme sports so unique and thrilling is that, more than anything else, they are battles against danger and the elements. Extreme sports like snowboarding, BMX biking, BASE (building, antenna, span, Earth) jumping, skateboarding, snow skiing, parkour, and many more all pit athletes against a combination of unpredictable weather, challenging obstacles, and the limitations of their own abilities.

There typically are no coaches, no high school teams, and no community youth programs that support young people interested in these sports, and the inherent danger involved with hitting a halfpipe full bore or tumbling down a mountain at speeds that would be illegal on many American roads are the biggest reasons why.

In other words, there are sports, and then there are extreme sports.

Unlike baseball, football, basketball, or most of the traditional sports enjoyed by millions of American athletes every day, extreme sports are much harder to classify because there simply are so many of them. Tony Hawk pushed skateboarding into the mainstream while Mat Hoffman and Dave Mirra revolutionized the world of freestyle BMX. Shaun White helped to bring snowboarding into the national spotlight. While these action sports are probably the most popular in the genre, there are scores of others, all of which require participants to conquer choppy waters, hilly terrains, frozen mountainsides, or the whipping winds that circle thousands of feet above the surface of the Earth.

ESPN's (the sports-oriented Entertainment and Sports Programming Network's) 1995 X Games, known then as the Extreme Games, helped to popularize the sports, while the 1999 introduction of the Extreme Sports Channel helped make these events more accessible to fans all over the world.

Today, there are tens of millions of young Americans participating in extreme sports, and the numbers keep on rising. With participation in more traditional sports dropping, it is clear the appeal of action sports is drawing people in as they continue to produce electrifying moments for fans.

Tony Hawk Dials Up the First-Ever 900 (1999)

If there's a Michael Jordan of extreme sports, it is Tony Hawk. The first time he ever landed the 900 (a 2.5-revolution aerial spin), it was the skateboarding equivalent of watching MJ stuff home his signature free-throw-line dunk. Up until 1999, nobody in the skateboarding world had ever successfully gotten all the way around for the full 2.5 spins, but at the X Games that year, Hawk finally nailed the 900 after failing his 10 previous attempts. He actually completed the trick after his allotted time had expired but won "Best Trick" anyway to the chagrin of some of his contemporaries, but had he not been allowed to continue (the announcers at the time joked, "We make up the rules as we go along!"), one of the most memorable moments in skateboarding history might never have happened.

Dave Mirra Lands a Double Backflip (2000)

BMX riders have been doing backflips on their bicycles for years, but when BMX legend Dave Mirra pulled off the first-ever double backflip in competition during the 2000 X Games, he proved why he is one of the greatest freestyle riders of all time. The trick was not entirely original at that point, as others already had pulled it off away from the bright lights of a competitive setting, but Mirra's having landed it at the sport's premier event was startling to fans. Mat Hoffman's no-handed 900 a couple of years later was equally impressive and staggering, but in 2000 it felt to some as if a new era of tougher tricks was on the horizon following Mirra's double backflip. Hoffman's impressive trick in 2002 proved that assumption was absolutely correct.

GREATEST MOMENTS

Bob Burnquist Flirts With Perfection (2001)

Known as one of skateboarding's most creative innovators, Burnquist is one of those rare athletes who knows what it feels like to knock on the door of perfection. Back in 2001 Burnquist absolutely owned the vert contest at that year's X Games. He entered his run in second place behind two-time defending champion Bucky Lasek and needed a huge score to topple the former winner. Burnquist, in what was the final pass of the event, assembled a near-flawless run, hitting a handful of tricks that had never been seen before and earning a score of 98, just about as close to perfection as any X Games athlete has ever been. Tony Hawk, who had been helping announce the historic run, screamed in disbelief throughout Burnquist's exhibition to the point where he was audibly hoarse by the end of it all.

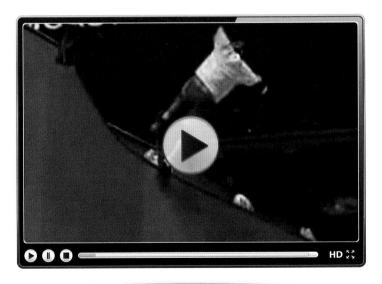

Brian Deegan Flips for FMX (2003)

A few years after the turn of the century, it seemed like an inevitability that somebody would eventually pull off a full front flip with a motocross bike as there were a number of athletes at that point pushing the limits of safety to prepare it for competition. Brian Deegan, however, was the man who actually did pull off the Mulisha Twist at the 2003 X Games, frustrating all those other FMX competitors who were holding the 360 in their pockets as a possible trick for their own routines. Deegan remains the most decorated freestyle motocross rider in history and has rebounded from horrifying injury, but back in 2003 his name was known best in the context of having been the first to achieve what was then the holy grail of FMX tricks.

Travis Pastrana Double Backflips His Way Into America's Heart (2006)

Pastrana was one of the bikers in 2003 who had considered attempting the flip trick that Deegan eventually owned, but Pastrana earned back his credibility three years later by shocking the motocross world with a trick many thought was impossible: the double backflip. Doing impossible things in the face of massive danger is what makes certain X Games moments legendary, and Pastrana put a lot of jaws on the floor when he landed a trick that just as easily could have killed him as make him a legend. No trick in this sport has been quite so awe-inspiring since.

Nyjah Huston Proves Age Is Nothing but a Number (2006)

By the time Nyjah Huston was 18 years old, he already had won more prize money than any other skateboarder in history, including Tony Hawk. A lot of that has to do with the fact that he made his official X Games debut in 2006 at age 11, by far the youngest person ever to compete there. He did not win that first year, but he did become the youngest gold medalist in X Games Skateboard Street history just a few years later at age 16. Back in 2006 Huston was just a wiry kid with flowing dreadlocks, but he has blossomed into quite an entrepreneur and one of the sport's most recognizable young stars. As an 11-year-old kid trying to find his away among the game's greats, the sky was the limit for Huston. Many years later, it still is.

GREATEST MOMENTS

James Kingston Takes Parkour to New Heights (2013)

By no means a household name, Kingston took the Internet by storm back in 2013, when he released videos of himself hanging one-handed from a crane 250 feet in the air and leaping all over the University of Cambridge's rooftops. While there are a number of ways to define parkour, freerunning is definitely the most common of them, and Kingston, with a GoPro camera strapped to his head, showed just how thrillingly dangerous the sport can be when taken to its highest heights. When university officials blasted Kingston for creating danger not only for himself but for others, he responded, "I didn't go up there to die; I went up there to live," which may be the most extreme thing a human being could have said in response to such criticism.

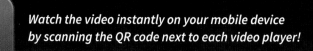

Danny MacAskill Rides the Ridge (2014)

While not as well-known as some of the bigger stars in the world of extreme sports, Danny MacAskill is an extremely talented trials cyclist from Scotland who generated a ton of YouTube views in 2014 for his intrepid ride along Cuillin Ridge, a tall, rocky series of cliffs located in MacAskill's home, the Isle of Skye. In just the first five days, the video of the ride, filmed by the BBC and titled "Riding the Ridge," garnered 10 million views. In just its first year, the anxiety-inducing video has nearly quadrupled that number. It certainly brings new meaning to the phrase "mountain biking."

Skateboarding's popularity soared to new heights in the 1970s and 1980s.

Words to Understand:

counterculture: a culture and lifestyle, usually among the young, that rejects or opposes the dominant values and behavior of society

exponentially: rising or expanding at an usually rapid rate

myriad: of an indefinitely great number, innumerable

CHAPTER 2

THE ORIGINS OF EXTREME SPORTS

There is no mysterious origin story for extreme sports. Many of the standard, modern activities in action sports were developed and popularized some time during the 1970s and 1980s, which is well within the confines of recorded history and so relatively easy to track.

OLD SCHOOL EXTREME

Of course, people have been climbing rocks, running long distances, and doing insane things on wheels for centuries, but only very recently have those efforts transformed into organized competitions that result in accolades and prize money. Motocross was perhaps the first of today's X Games events to have found widespread popularity as a sport as the first motorcycle races occurred almost immediately following the invention of the motorcycle itself. Some documented races kicked off shortly after the turn of the century, but by the 1920s the sport had evolved into something considerably more civil and widespread. Over time it progressed into what it is today.

Beyond the humble beginnings of motocross, many experts agree that the first extreme sports, at least in the modern sense of the distinction, were rock climbing and marathon running, two activities that grew **exponentially** in popularity during the early 1970s. That is not surprising considering the counterculture atmosphere that existed in an era where a movement began among young people in Western culture who were growing bored with what they considered to be the safe, complacent lifestyle adhered to by their parents' generation.

Motocross is the oldest of the group of activities now classified as extreme or action sports.

GIVE US DANGER

Mere running and climbing would not satisfy the **counterculture** need for danger and adrenaline for long. By 1979, a group of Oxford students created an organization called the Dangerous Sports Club of Oxford University, which was put together with the intention of seriously pushing the limits of human safety. In fact, these were the people who invented modern bungee jumping and gleefully plunged from bridges all over England in an attempt to feel the rush of adrenaline they craved in their lives before founding their controversial club. Later forays into BASE jumping and hang gliding inside of active volcanoes only solidified the group's role in introducing the world to extreme sports culture.

THE CLASSICS

It was during the late 1970s and 1980s when things really took off, however, as that was the era in which skateboarding, snowboarding, and BMX riding all rode to prominence in the world of extreme sports.

Modern bungee jumping was invented in England by members of the Dangerous Sports Club of Oxford University.

The origins of all three extend well beyond those decades as bicycle racing obviously has been around for centuries, and both snowboarding and skateboarding were inspired by surfing, a much older action sport all its own. The freestyle iterations of these sports, however, are much more modern takes on long-existing wheeled and board-based forms of thrill-seeking. They are the activities that fuel the danger-filled culture of the extreme sports generation.

Empty swimming pools were the first skate parks for skateboarders in drought-stricken California in the late 1970s.

INTO THE DEEP END

Skateboarding, for example, famously got its start in the late 1970s, when a drought in California forced homeowners to drain their pools. Teenagers with boards looked at every empty concrete pit as a challenge to be overcome, and it was during that era when skateboarders started using their boards in different ways and inventing **myriad** new tricks.

By the 1980s, skateboarders were grinding handrails and frequenting brand-new skate parks to hone their craft. As the sport grew into the 1990s, it was not long before skateboard equipment and merchandise companies recognized the marketing opportunities around sponsoring the sport's most important up-and-coming stars.

BIKES AND BOARDS

The story for freestyle BMX is not all that different. In 1975, California teens rode their bikes in the concrete Escondido reservoir channels and, eventually, skate parks while trying out bicycle tricks that had never been attempted previously. Like the enterprising skateboarders, BMX riders also took advantage of empty pools, which were early forms of the street and vert events that are so popular today.

As for snowboarding, no one origin story applies to the invention of the modern snowboard, but all of those entrepreneurs that developed snow versions of surfboards seemed to have had the same idea at right around the same time: surfing in the snow would be incredibly fun. Mass-produced snowboards were a little slower to come than skateboards and BMX bicycles, but by 1981 there were official snowboard contests happening regularly. It would take fewer than 20 more years for it to become an Olympic event.

A BMX rider performs the tailwhip air trick.

There are, of course, rich histories behind every extreme sport, from surfing to endurance running to skydiving and BASE jumping. It is the diversity of their origin stories that is a big part of what makes extreme sports so interesting. In some form, they have been around forever, but the really interesting thing is that as organized sports, they all are only just getting off the ground.

 Text-Dependent Questions:

1. What was the first of today's X Games events to have found widespread popularity as a sport?

2. In 1979, what student group was put together with the intention of seriously pushing the limits of human safety?

3. How did skateboarding famously get its start in the late 1970s?

 Research Project:

Take a look at the stories behind the individuals who are credited with bringing extreme sports into the spotlight. What were their motivations? Did they gain notoriety in the same way as the men who are known for starting football, baseball, or golf? What role did each person play in the development of the sport?

Racers jump 30 feet in the air at speeds of more than 60 mph in the SnoCross event at the Winter X Games.

Words to Understand:

BASE jumping: a parachute jump from the top of a building, bridge, or cliff, usually at a height of 1,000 feet (305 meters) or less

inline skating: a roller skate typically with four hard-rubber wheels in a straight line resembling the blade of an ice skate

ultramarathon: a footrace longer than a marathon

CHAPTER 3

TYPES OF EXTREME SPORTS

Variety is the name of the game when it comes to extreme sports, which really are more like a roster of Olympic events than any one individual activity. Athletes who participate in these sometimes death-defying pursuits have many options from which to choose, most of which pit them against one element or another.

THE TOP 10

In general, land sports are the most popular among American youths, with the top four in terms of participation involving activities that are performed mostly outdoors in warm weather. According to the Sporting Good Manufacturer's Association (SGMA) International's analysis of the Superstudy® of Sports Participation, inline skating (17.4 million participants), skateboarding (11.6 million participants), paintball (9.6 million participants), and artificial wall climbing (7.7 million participants) are currently the most popular extreme sports in the United States, which should not be surprising considering those are very often the most accessible, affordable, and relatively safe action sports that currently exist.

Other activities in the top 10 include snowboarding (7.1 million), trail running (6.5 million), mountain biking (5.3 million), wakeboarding (2.8 million), BMX bicycling (2.6 million), and rock climbing (2.1 million). Once again, the majority of these are generally safe activities, but that does not mean that there are not more challenging and more dangerous options out there for hungry athletes hunting for a challenge.

Free soloing is the sport of rock climbing without the safety of ropes or harnesses.

TAKING IT UP A NOTCH

BASE jumping and skydiving, for example, come with quite a bit of inherent danger, as do the freestyle versions of sports like skateboarding, BMX, snowboarding, motocross, and others. Then there's "creeking," a form of canoeing and kayaking that places an individual into low-flow whitewater rapids, and there are some that consider it the most dangerous extreme sport in the world because of the risks of getting trapped underwater or smashing into a series of jagged rocks.

Free soloing, a form of outdoor rock climbing that does not use harnesses or ropes, is another activity that presents plenty of built-in risk, which is why there are few people in the world that partake in it. Most of the best rock climbers in the world, even those who love the thrill of the world's most stimulating ascents, would not dare abandon their safety fallbacks, but there simply are some people who just want to make their extreme activities as extreme as possible.

EMBRACING THE ELEMENTS

Regardless of danger, there are a few different ways that extreme sports can be organized. Some view them as activities that require the use of vehicles versus those that do not, while others would rather classify them by element: earth, water, air, or snow.

Snow- and ice-based sports, including snowboarding, snow skiing, snowmobiling, ice climbing, and others are what serve as the foundation of the Winter X Games. The winter version is a significantly smaller event than what ESPN puts together for the Summer X Games, which feature many of the more popular action sports, like skateboarding, motocross, mountain biking, BMX, rally car racing, and off-road trucking. **Inline skating**, climbing, bungee jumping, skysurfing, and water sports like wakeboarding and barefoot waterski jumping also have been part of Summer X Games in the past.

BEYOND EXTREME

Not all extreme sports are celebrated at the X Games, however. Distance biking and **ultramarathon** running take entirely too much time to be enjoyed with any level of excitement by an audience that typically tunes in for skateboard tricks and motocross races. An ultramarathon, any footrace longer than the standard 26.219 miles, can take days to complete. While an activity requiring that level of stamina and training absolutely falls under the banner of "extreme," it simply is not as exciting as watching someone jump from a plane or get the biggest of big air on any of a number of extreme sports vehicles.

The truth is that the definition of what qualifies as an extreme sport expands every year, with new and exciting options presenting themselves all the time. River bugging, for example, is a relatively new activity that has participants use "paddle mitts" rather than an actual paddle to maneuver down rapids in a kayak. Skishing is another new one that puts fishermen (or fisherwomen) on skis and forces them to reel in a big fish, while the hooked river dweller pulls them along for the ensuing ride. Powerski jetboarding involves a 45-horsepower surfboard capable of reaching speeds upward of 45 miles per hour (72.4 km/h), which is both exhilarating and extremely challenging.

What new types of extreme sports will present themselves in the future? That is impossible to know, but according to participation data, inline skating is now significantly more popular than baseball among American youths. That kind of popularity will not be the trend for all types of extreme sports, but the fact is that playing extreme is becoming extremely common for young Americans.

In River Bugging, athletes use paddle mitts to maneuver through rapids in a specially designed watercraft.

 ## Text-Dependent Questions:

1. According to SGMA International's analysis of the Superstudy® of Sports Participation, which four sports are currently the most popular extreme sports in the United States?

2. Name two extreme sports that come with the possibility of the most inherent danger.

3. What are three of the newest extreme sports?

Research Project:

Create a chart showing the top 10 extreme sports and where they are most practiced in the United States. Now note the climate, demographics, physical conditions, and so on in each of these areas. What is your analysis for why some sports are more prevalent in certain parts of the country?

Many people think skydiving (right) is a dangerous activity, but the extreme sport of BASE jumping (left) is 53 times more deadly.

Words to Understand:

precarious: dependent on chance circumstances, unknown conditions, or uncertain developments

traverse: to cross or lie across

mantra: a word or phrase that is repeated often or that expresses someone's basic beliefs

CHAPTER 4

THE DRAW OF DANGER

Extreme sports are dangerous, so much so, in fact, that more than 4 million people were injured while participating in extreme sports between 2000 and 2011, according to the National Electronic Injury Surveillance System.

DEFYING DEATH

Furthermore, around 2.5 percent of extreme sports injuries are severe or life threatening, and according to data collected by Oxford University, the odds of dying in a BASE jumping accident (1 in 2,317 jumps) are much higher than the odds of dying in a car accident, proving the danger quotient of some of the more **precarious** extreme sports.

High-profile deaths like those of freeskiier Sarah Burke, climber Dean Potter, and BASE jumper Eric Roner remind action sports athletes and fans that even the best in the business can fail tragically at their crafts. While brushes with death are not everyday occurrences for any extreme athlete, 72 percent of BASE jumpers have admitted to witnessing the death or serious injury of other participants, and 76 percent of them admitted to having had at least one "near-miss" incident, according to Discovery News.

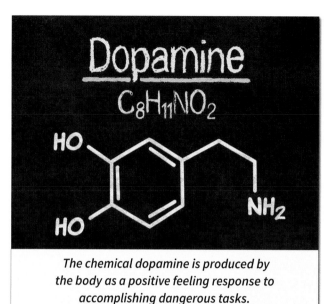

The chemical dopamine is produced by the body as a positive feeling response to accomplishing dangerous tasks.

A CHEMICAL ROMANCE

Knowing this, it is a small miracle that athletes continue to jump from planes, **traverse** terrain at entirely unsafe speeds, and flip heavy equipment upside down, but extreme athletes are not dissuaded by the risk of bodily harm. In fact, there is plenty of science that proves the threat of danger is a big reason why extreme athletes keep coming back for more punishment.

According to Popular Social Science, dopamine is a key neurotransmitter that controls the part of the brain responsible for motivating human beings. When an athlete survives a close call or, even better, successfully completes a challenging yet dangerous task, dopamine kicks in and sends positive feelings throughout the body. It is the same way that some drugs work, so to call this sort of chemical reaction a "high" actually would be entirely appropriate.

FEAR IS THE ONLY OPTION

"There's an innate characteristic in some people," said Justin Anderson, PsyD, a sports consultant for the Center for Sports Psychology in Denton, Texas, in an interview with WebMD. "Some people are turned on by that stuff; they get a lot of adrenaline by it, and they gravitate toward activities that give them that feeling. For some it's jumping out of airplanes, for others it's climbing Mt. Everest, and for others, it's the Ironman (triathlon) race. When they find that sport or activity that gives them that feeling, they say there is nothing better."

In other words, these athletes are not driven by a "no fear" **mantra**; rather, it is the presence of that fear that ultimately results in the pleasure one gets from surviving a dangerous activity.

LOFTY GOALS

Adrenaline is not the only reason extreme athletes participate in their sports, however. Others derive a deep satisfaction from setting a seemingly impossible goal and then working to achieve it. For many extreme athletes, the training is just as enjoyable as the performance itself, although finally seeing the fruit of the labor is the ultimate reward for all the hard work.

"Competing in the Ironman is solely for me," said Rick Hall, a registered dietician who also competes in other very challenging races. "It's the ability to say I've done it. It's pushing my body to its absolute limits. I'm competitive in nature, in life, and business, but when it comes to competing as an athlete at the Ironman level, it's about self-competition, and how well I can do, and what my personal best can be."

Adrenaline

$C_9H_{13}NO_3$

The term "adrenaline junkie" alludes to the chemical being addictive. The chemical produced by the body at times of stress and fear is responsible for that "rush" many extreme athletes experience.

MAN VERSUS WORLD

One thing that sets some extreme sports apart from more traditional varieties is that many of them require athletes to compete against themselves and the elements rather than other people. It is a different sort of competition that calls on them to be self-driven, resilient, and in many cases independent, so the appeal of activities like skateboarding, rock climbing, motocross, skydiving, or any other action sport is that they provide exactly this kind of outlet for individuals.

Adrenaline and dopamine drive these athletes on a chemical level, but the thrill of a challenge can be equally intoxicating for some. Yes, extreme sports are dangerous, but danger is not necessarily what motivates these people. Rather, it is a desire to be the best at something, to better one's self and to own the elements.

THE NEXT STEP

"I love that pursuit of progression, trying to overcome something that scared me and accomplishing what I had set out to do," said wakeboarding star Danny Harf. "Succeed or fail, it's about getting outside of your comfort zone. The only way to go forward is to be willing to take that next step."

To take that next step, ignoring fear must be part of the equation, even if there is plenty to be afraid of.

The dangers of extreme sports are part of the appeal for action sports athlete.

Text-Dependent Questions:

1. According to data collected by Oxford University, the odds of dying in a BASE jumping accident are much higher than the odds of dying in what other kind of accident?

2. What is a key neurotransmitter that controls the part of the brain responsible for motivating human beings?

3. Why do extreme sports athletes take these dangerous risks? What motivates them?

 # Research Project:

Take a closer look at how dopamine and adrenaline affect your body, and investigate how these chemicals can be so vastly different in individuals.

Brian Deegan at X Games 17 in Los Angeles competes in the Moto X Step Up event.

Words to Understand:

unequivocal: very strong and clear, not showing or allowing any doubt

biennial: taking place every other year

biathlon: an event in which athletes ski over the countryside and stop to shoot rifles at target

CHAPTER 5

THE X GAMES AND THE OLYMPICS

While there are multiple reasons that extreme sports have become so popular among modern athletes, the exposure generated by the X Games and then later acceptance by the Olympic Games both have played arguably the most significant parts in directing these activities toward larger audiences.

EXTREME GAMES

It all started in 1995 with ESPN's Extreme Games; a televised event meant not only to showcase the best in what was then a burgeoning world of action sports but also to capitalize on a growing section of young consumers who simply were not interested in many of the more traditional sports. By introducing what a USA Today newspaper columnist at the time called the "Look Ma, No Hands! Olympics," ESPN was providing a broadcast outlet for a growing number of youths who loved skateboarding while also widening their own viewership beyond the typical baseball, football, basketball, and hockey fans.

Street luging was one of the original events at ESPN's Extreme Games in 1995.

Those first Extreme Games in Newport, Rhode Island, were an **unequivocal** success for the network, with more than 500,000 people showing up to watch stars like Tony Hawk and Mat Hoffman in person and hundreds of thousands more tuning in on television. The exhibition was more diverse in the mid-1990s than it is now, with now-defunct eventslike inline skating, bungee jumping, skysurfing, and even street luging showcasing participants during that first go-around, but it was enough to capture the fascination of the country, which helped inspire ESPN to bring it back the following year.

CALIFORNIA LOVE

That is saying something considering the sports network's original plan was to organize the Extreme Games only once every two years, like a **biennial** hard-core Olympics, but when 1996's rechristened "X Games" proved just as popular, ESPN knew it was onto something. Those games also took place in Rhode Island, but it would not be long before the events followed their destiny and expanded westward, especially when the decision was made to also feature a Winter X Games focusing on sports like snowboarding and skiing.

With excitement and interest building over the increased success of both the Summer and Winter X Games, ESPN eventually turned its attention to California, which served as home to both events through 1999. In those important first handful of years, Hawk, Hoffman, Mirra, and Pastrana made household names of themselves and helped turn the X Games from a lightly regarded sideshow of extreme sports freaks into one of the most hotly anticipated sporting exhibitions of the year.

OLYMPIC EXPOSURE

As these events gained credibility around the turn of the century, the International Olympic Committee (IOC) took notice and somewhat surprisingly decided to adopt a few X Games events into their own arsenal of sports competitions, with snowboarding being the first to gain medal status from the IOC in 1998 for the halfpipe and parallel giant slalom events. BMX racing was added in 2008, whereas nontraditional skiing earned its first events in 2014.

Clearly, the IOC is learning the lesson that ESPN learned two decades earlier: younger viewers are more interested in winter extreme sports events and bored by traditional events like curling or the **biathlon**. In 2014 alone, 9 of the 14 new events added to the slate at the Winter Games in Sochi were either snowboarding or nontraditional skiing events, and there is little evidence to suggest that this trend will not continue with future Summer Olympic Games.

Ladies' Halfpipe Qualification at the Sochi 2014 XXII Olympic Winter Games

EXTREME IS MAINSTREAM

In fact, there is a strong push for skateboarding, surfing, and sport climbing to be included in the 2020 Summer Olympics in Tokyo, Japan. Shaun White and Tony Hawk both have been predictably vocal about skateboarding's inclusion, and it would appear that the Tokyo 2020 organizing committee is taking all three potential new events quite seriously, according to the British Broadcasting Corporation (BBC). Sport climbing already was a demonstration sport at the Youth Olympic Games in Nanjing, China, back in 2014. There is no reason that skateboarding and surfing should not earn the same respect that snowboarding and freestyle skiing have earned in the Winter Olympic Games.

Knowing that there is a need for more star power in both Olympic events, as well as a desire to draw in more and younger viewers, it should not come as a huge surprise that the IOC has adopted many of the events that have made both the X Games and extreme sports in general so widespread and adored.

The X Games themselves, meanwhile, are not going anywhere, as they continue to be a marketing coup and ratings success for ESPN, and as long as that endures, more incentive will exist for the IOC to continue adding action sport events to its own roster of medal competitions. Organizers are discovering that, like any event, these sports can be enjoyed by those who do not participate in them just as easily as they are enjoyed by those who do, and these televised events continue to provide entertainment for both groups.

A skateboarder performs an air trick during an afternoon workout at Venice Skatepark, Venice Beach, California.

 Text-Dependent Questions:

1. When was ESPN's first Extreme Games televised?

2. What was the first extreme sport to gain medal status from the IOC in 1998?

3. There is a strong push for which three sports to be included in the 2020 Summer Olympics in Tokyo, Japan?

Research Project:

Compare the numbers. How many viewers watch the X Games, and how many watch these sports televised during the Olympics? How much does it cost an advertiser to run a commercial during the X Games versus extreme sports events during the Olympics? What kinds of endorsement deals do extreme athletes secure versus athletes of older, more conventional sports such as football, baseball, or basketball? Compare and contrast the money behind the sports.

Shaun White

Words to Understand:

apexes: the tops or highest points of something

sojourn: a period of time when you stay in a place as a traveler or guest

juggernaut: something that is extremely large and powerful and cannot be stopped

CHAPTER

THE STARS

World-famous extreme sports stars do exist, and their names are just as well or better known than those of Tom Brady, LeBron James, Sidney Crosby, and Mike Trout. Tony Hawk is a skateboarding icon on the level of Michael Jordan, and Shaun White's name is known not only by snowboarding fans but by casual sports fans as well. Beyond these mainstream crossover stars, however, lies a host of talented and widely respected action sports athletes that continue to do some truly amazing things.

White obviously is the most important of today's active stars, earning as much as $20 million a year in winnings and endorsements, all of which is justified considering how much he's accomplished in both snowboarding and skateboarding. Not only does White currently hold the record for the most Winter X Games gold and overall medals, but he also has seen crossover success by winning gold in the halfpipe at both the 2006 Turin Winter Olympics and the 2010 Vancouver Winter Olympics. White was a snowboarding prodigy at age 6 and earned his first sponsorship deal only a year later. At age 9 skateboarding legend Tony Hawk took him under his wing, and that helped push White to turn pro as a skateboarder by age 17. Everything else from that point on is extreme sports history as White continues to dominate events and help push the sport into the mainstream.

Tony Hawk

While anybody can pay a few hundred bucks to strap themselves to a professional skydiver and jump out of an airplane, Jeb Corliss has over the course of his career gone out of his way to demonstrate that skydiving and BASE jumping are not intended to be that safe. No human being on the face of the planet has taken as many risks as a BASE jumper as Corliss, a man who has successfully leapt from the **apexes** of the Eifel Tower in Paris, France, the Space Needle in Seattle, Washington, the Christ the Redeemer statue in Rio de Janeiro, Brazil, and the Petronas Twin Towers in Kuala Lumpur, Malaysia. In 2006, he attempted to BASE jump off of the Empire State Building with a camera strapped to his head but was caught, restrained, and arrested by the New York Police Department. Corliss is a daredevil in every sense of the word and continues to push the sport of BASE jumping to new heights, literally.

Austrian skydiver Felix Baumgartner is best known for donning a spacesuit in October of 2012 and dropping 24 miles (39 km) to the Earth in what proved at that point to be the highest skydive in history. The YouTube video of the attempt is dizzying as Baumgartner freefalls all those miles above the face of the Earth, and knowing that he raced toward New Mexico at a record-breaking 843.6 miles per hour (1,357.64 km/h) makes the attempt all the more impressive. In fact, during that jump Baumgartner became the first human being to break the sound barrier outside of a moving vehicle. Much of his fame has come from this jump, but he's a well-rounded skydiver and BASE jumper and was known for his risky stunts even before his **sojourn** into the stratosphere. With a viral Internet video to help keep his legacy alive, Baumgartner has become something of a household name.

Proof positive that extreme sports athletes don't have to be crazy to do what they do, Lizzy Hawker is a gutsy endurance runner with a Ph.D. in physical oceanography, although she certainly is better known for her unbelievably long and challenging runs than she is for her academic prowess. In 2005, she bought her first pair of trail running shoes and then 10 days later won the Ultra-Trail du Mont-Blanc, a 103-mile trek through the Alps in France, Italy,

Felix Baumgartner

Lizzy Hawker

and Switzerland. A year later, she won the International Association of Ultrarunners (IAU) 62-mile (100 km) World Championships, and in 2007 she ran 199 miles (320 km) from the Mount Everest South Base Camp to Kathmandu, Nepal, in a record 77 hours, 36 minutes. Hawker also holds the world record for distance running in 24 hours with 153.5 miles (247 km) as well as the women's record for completing the 155-mile (249 km) Spartathalon. In 2015, showing no signs of slowing down, she ran 994 miles (1,600 km) across the Himalayas in Nepal.

Kelly Slater isn't the young, burgeoning star he once was, but well into his 40s, he still is an active big-wave surfer and remains arguably the most recognizable name in his sport. No human being has won the Association of Surfing Professionals World Tour (now known as the World Surf League Tour [WSL]) more than Slater's 11 times, and the span between his first title, won at age 20, and his most recent one at age 39 is the widest of any other surfer in history by a staggering amount. Today, he is the all-time leader in career event wins and in 2015 was ranked seventh by the WSL, an impressive feat considering he was one of only two surfers over the age of 27 ranked in the top 10 and the only surfer over the age of 35. Even as he gets older, Slater remains one of the most dominant athletes in surfing.

Gus Kenworthy has been dominating Association of Freeskiing Professional (AFP) World Tour events almost from the moment he turned pro, winning the AFP World Championships overall titles in 2011, 2012, and 2013. Those titles only served as the beginning for what would prove to be a dominant career. Kenworthy went on to win a bronze medal in slopestyle for his first Winter X Games in 2013 and a silver medal at the Winter Olympic Games in Sochi, Russia, in 2014, where he performed as an openly gay athlete in a country with official antihomosexual policies. Throughout 2015, he further improved his standing as the greatest freeskier in the world by dominating tournaments with unbelievable strings and combinations of tricks. With more X Games and the 2018 Winter Olympics forthcoming, he should only solidify himself as the most dominant athlete in his sport.

Kelly Slater

Gus Kenworthy

Tucker Hibbert   Jamie Bestwick   Chris Sharma

Widely considered to be among the best rock climbers in the world, Chris Sharma truly defines extreme sports with his combination of sheer athleticism, risk taking, and dominance over Mother Nature, all of which he has proven by tackling some of the hardest climbs any human being has ever undertaken. He started climbing in high school and by age 14 already was attempting some of the more challenging obstacles in the sport. In the two decades since, Sharma has toppled many of the world's toughest ascents, including Necessary Evil at the Virgin River Gorge in Arizona, the Mandala in California, Biographie in France, La Rambla in Spain, and Jumbo Love at Clark Mountain in California. He screams like a maniac during his climbs, but it's hard to blame him considering their difficulty.

There never has been a more accomplished athlete in the sport of snocross than Tucker Hibbert. Snocross is a Winter X Games event that puts high-performance snowmobiles onto challenging racetracks and dares riders to beat the best in the business. Since 2007, however, beating the best has proven impossible, as Hibbert has taken home the gold medal in every Winter X Games. In fact, since 2000 he's failed to medal at all only twice (2001 and 2006), and up until 2015 he was the youngest gold medal winner in Winter X Games history. He, of course, has seen success away from those events as well, winning the U.S. National Snocross championship eight times and the FIM Snocross World Championship twice. Few extreme athletes have ever dominated their event so thoroughly.

Nyjah Huston   *Juliana Buhring*

Some extreme athletes simply dominate single events and make entire careers out of making the competition look second-rate. That is the case with Jamie Bestwick, a BMX vert **juggernaut** who has absolutely owned his event for well over a decade. In 2015, he was relegated to the silver medal at the X Games after having won gold in the BMX vert event for nine consecutive years, and it was he who dethroned Dave Mirra, his predecessor in the event and a BMX legend, which led to a long career of trophies and medals for a guy who started riding BMX bikes as a 10-year-old youth in the United Kingdom.

At only 20 years old, Nyjah Huston is one of extreme sports' most promising rising stars as he already has won more prize money skateboarding than anybody else in history. He is remarkably decorated for being as young as he is, having won gold in street at the X Games four of the last five years and being named overall champion at the Street League Skateboarding Competition three of the last four years. He is a true rising star in extreme sports and looks primed to own the sport for years, possibly decades, to come.

In Jules Verne's famous novel, Around the World in 80 Days, Phileas Fogg attempts to circumnavigate the globe in a hot-air balloon in an unreasonable measure of time. Distance cycler Juliana Buhring attempted a similar journey on her bicycle in 2012 and ultimately broke the record as the fastest woman to bike around the world, although it did take her 152 days (144 of which were spent riding) to get it done. The following year she participated in the first-ever transcontinental race through the Alps and finished ninth despite being the only woman to enter. Buhring defines endurance and is considered one of the premier extreme athletes in the world.

Kelly Slater competes in the Quiksilver Pro at Snapper Rocks Coolangatta Gold Coast, Australia.

Text-Dependent Questions:

1. Which snowboarding sensation earns as much as $20 million a year in winnings and endorsements?

2. Who is widely considered to be among the best rock climbers in the world?

3. Which snocross athlete has taken home the gold medal in every Winter X Games since 2007?

 Research Project:

Some researchers believe that people with certain personality traits are more likely to participate in high-risk activities such as extreme sports. Pick five of the stars mentioned in this chapter, and look closer at their personalities and lives. Is there a connection between them in terms of personality traits? How about demographics? Examine why they choose to participate in such high-risk sports, despite the element of danger.

RICKY CARMICHAEL

SARAH BURKE

DANNY WAY

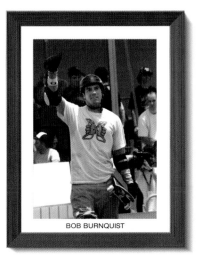
BOB BURNQUIST

MAT HOFFMAN

TRAVIS PASTRANA

SHAUN WHITE   RODNEY MULLEN   JEREMY MCGRATH

KELLY CLARK

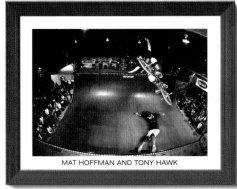
MAT HOFFMAN AND TONY HAWK

VICKI GOLDEN

BOB HANNAH

In 1995, sports network ESPN debuted the Extreme Games, a collection of events based on action sports. For the first time, events like skateboarding, street luge, BMX riding and barefoot water skiing got mainstream exposure. The broadcast was a huge success, and the event returned the following year rebranded as the X Games. Marketed as "sheer unadulterated athletic lunacy", the X Games spawned a winter version in 1997, and over the decades have become a refined and well-organized marketing machine that attracts top sponsors and makes stars of action sports athletes.

CHAPTER

EXTREME SPORTS' GREATEST ATHLETES

Like many Olympic events, extreme sports like those that occur at the X Games every year are very often scored subjectively. It is nowhere near as rigid a scoring system as those in place for, say, figure skating or gymnastics, but these are events where judges decide which athlete is hitting criteria most effectively, and that means that the difference between a gold medal and a silver one often is a result of a handful of judges' opinions.

Despite this subjectivity, it's not necessarily challenging to determine which extreme athletes are among the greatest of all time because those who impress judges year after year clearly can offer enough by way of new and exciting tricks to remain relevant over long stretches of time. The legends in freestyle action sports are the ones with the talent and longevity to stay fresh, which can prove challenging considering all the fresh, young talent that pops onto the scene every year as these sports become more popular.

Not all X Games events are determined by judges, however; several are matters of athletes reaching the highest heights or rattling off the quickest times. There are races, too, that make it even easier to determine which athletes are the best in their respective businesses.

Just like with the Olympics, the X Games hand out gold, silver, and bronze medals, although there are plenty of other non-televised action sports events that reward winners with trophies or prize money instead. How much money and what sort of accolade depend entirely on the event, but there are plenty of them, and each has its legends—men and women who have blazed trails for their sports and blazed the competition in the process.

Mega ramp skateboarding in Rio de Janeiro

SKATEBOARDING

While there is no official "Father of Skateboarding," Rodney Mullen certainly comes the closest. After getting his start in skateboarding in the late 1970s, he would go on to invent an unbelievable number of the sport's most iconic tricks, including the flatground ollie, airwalk, kickflip, sidewinder, heelflip, impossible, and 360-flip, among many, many others. The early 1980s belonged to him and him alone, and without his innovations, both vert and street skateboarding would not be what they are today.

An essential pioneer in the development of street skateboarding, Mark Gonzales long has been considered one of the most influential skaters in the history of the sport. One of his more notable firsts was skateboarding on handrails before anybody else had thought or tried to do so, but he has won innumerable street competitions in his decades on a board. As a teenager in the early 1980s, "Gonz" found his way in a budding counterculture activity that proved a perfect fit for someone who in 2011 would be named Transworld Skateboarding Magazine's "Most Influential Skateboarder of All Time."

Today, Tony Hawk is well-known and handsomely paid for his best-selling video game franchise, but in the 1980s and 1990s he was the most famous and most dominant skateboarder in the world. His list of contest wins is extensive and varied, with first-place finishes and gold medals in events all over the world. He retired from professional competitions in 1999, so he had only a few years to participate in those first few X Games, but even then he took home a number of gold medals. He parlayed his success into lucrative skateboarding-based business ventures. Both in terms of money and accolades, there might not be a more successful extreme athlete every to have lived.

One of the more extreme skateboarders in the history of the sport, some of Danny Way's most memorable moments include dropping onto a ramp from a helicopter and mega-ramping over the Great Wall of China. On top of stunts like this, Way is incredibly decorated, having won numerous big air medals at the X Games from 1995 to 2008. He has broken his neck and had 13 operations, but that is the price a man pays for legend status.

As far as X Games skateboarders are concerned, few have been as successful over time as Bob Burnquist has been and continues to be. He was the first skater to land the fakie 900 trick and one of only five people breathing to have completed the 900 at all, but his real claim to fame is his record 29 medals (including 14 gold medals) won at various X Games events between 1997 and 2015. He seems to be an ageless competitor who apparently grows better the older he gets. No X Games athlete is more decorated.

Rodney Mullen

Mark Gonzales

Tony Hawk

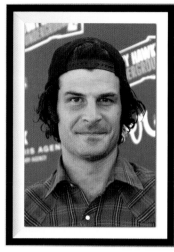
Mat Hoffman

Dave Mirra

Garrett Reynolds

BMX

Back in 1987 the idea of a 15-year-old kid joining the BMX circuit was ludicrous, but that's exactly what Mat Hoffman did, and he immediately took that world by storm. A few years later he branched out as an entrepreneur, starting Hoffman Bikes and Hoffman Promotions, which were largely responsible for the establishment of the Bicycle Stunt Series, one of the early stages for BMX riders to showcase their talents. He's an elite performer as well, with X Games medals to his name, but it's what he did around the sport for so long that has made him one of BMX's most revered personalities.

When it comes to BMX, there might not be a name more recognizable in the sport than Dave Mirra, a man who has hauled in obscene numbers of X Games medals and helped make his events among the most popular in extreme sports. For years, he held more X Games medals than anybody else in history (24) but was only recently surpassed by Bob Burnquist. His work in vert and park riding made him legendary in the business, and he pushed the envelope up until his tragic suicide in 2016 at age 41. In the aftermath of his death, the mayor of the town where Mirra lived in North Carolina suggested he may have suffered from chronic traumatic encephalopathy (CTE), a brain disease brought on by repeated concussions. Greenville mayor Allan Thomas was a friend of Mirra's and speculated that Mirra may have been depressed, which is a clinical feature of CTE. Although research is ongoing, especially due to the high-profile suicides of several ex-professional football players in recent years, no conclusive science linking CTE to suicide has been found.

Fox Racing calls Nina Buitrago "hands down the most influential woman in BMX," and her résumé goes a long way toward confirming that. She was the first woman to grind a handrail on a BMX and, in fact, has made a career besting male riders in competitions in a sport where female competitions still are a relatively new endeavor. She has won countless contests and once was named one of ESPN's "20 Most Unstoppable Women in Action Sports." There are male BMX riders who would do anything to boast her skill set.

Already considered to be one of the best street riders ever, Garrett Reynolds is just now entering his prime as an X Games legend. He has won six of the seven BMX street contests he's participated in at the X Games and has been named the Number One Rider Award (NORA) Cup Street Rider of the Year six separate times. As good as he is, it's scary to think just how much better he will get before the competition part of his career is over.

When it comes to BMX Vert, no name is more synonymous than that of UK star Jamie Bestwick. At home on a bike since the age of 10, Bestwick only rode BMX for fun, graduating from school to a career as an airline mechanic. The lure of competition would prove to be too strong, however, and Bestwick started riding full time. He became the dominant rider of his generation, winning nine straight X Games golds in Vert at one point and 13 golds overall.

MOTOCROSS

Perhaps the first real mainstream star in the world of motocross, Bob "Hurricane" Hannah is an all-time legend with 70 American Motorcyclist Association (AMA) National wins and seven AMA National Championships to his name. He also is one of only two motocross racers ever to have won championships in both 125cc and 250cc motocross and Supercross, proving his versatility and dominance in the sport. There was no greater rider in the 1970s, and Hannah still holds up as one of the greatest riders of all time.

Few motocross champions have ever been quite as popular as Jeremy McGrath, the man who dominated the 1990s like Bob Hannah had done two decades earlier. McGrath won a record 72 main events in 250cc and won seven 250cc Supercross championships between 1993 and 2000. He also won a couple of 125cc AMA Western Region Supercross Championships and one 250cc AMA National Motocross Championship, while amassing a total of 89 career AMA wins. Few motocross riders can even come close to matching that list of career highlights.

Eventually, Ricky Carmichael grabbed the metaphorical torch from McGrath, taking over the sport in the late 1990s and early 2000s to a level where some consider him to be the "GOAT," or "Greatest of All Time" in motocross. Known as something of a reckless driver, Carmichael has a list of achievements a mile long, including X Games gold medals in motocross racing and Motocross Step-Up. In 2015, he was inducted into the Motorsports Hall of Fame of America, solidifying himself as an all-time great.

Arguably the most popular motocross rider in the sport's history, Travis Pastrana is an adrenaline junkie who has seen success in motocross, rally cars, and even NASCAR. If it has wheels and goes fast, Pastrana has probably driven it, although the overwhelming majority of his success, and what made him famous, has been his work in motocross. With 8 X Games gold medals and 13 medals overall, Pastrana is a highly decorated freestyle motocross driver with talent and charm to match his success.

While only in her 20s, Vicki Golden already has established herself as the most notable female driver in motocross. Put "The first woman to . . ." in front of anything involving motocross, and it probably has something to do with Golden, who has three gold medals in women's motocross racing at the X Games and plenty of strong finishes even in otherwise all-male events. Women have not always been given opportunities to excel in typically male extreme sports activities like motocross, but Golden has proven that "riding like a girl" is something toward which to strive.

Jeremy McGrath

Ricky Carmichael

Travis Pastrana

Sarah Burke

Shaun White

Tanner Hall

EXTREME WINTER SPORTS

Considered by many to be one of the founding fathers of extreme sports, Shaun Palmer is the man who helped launch mainstream snowboarding. He has a gold medal for the sport at the X Games every year between 1997 and 2002, but also owns medals from the Gravity Games, the Snowboard World Cup, the Swatch World Halfpipe Championship, the World Championships, and the U.S. National Championships. In 1998, he was named "World's Greatest Athlete" by USA Today and even was named to the 2006 Winter Olympics snowboarding team, although he did not compete due to an injury. Shaun White is extreme sports' megastar today, but Shaun Palmer set the table for White's success.

Shaun White simply has been one of the most famous and beloved action sports stars of all time. He has earned 13 gold medals at the X Games in a decade of competition as well as 2 gold medals at the 2006 and 2010 Winter Olympics, but that only shows a small swath of his success, which simply has been unparalleled, not only in snowboarding but in skateboarding, for which he owns 5 more X Games medals, 2 of which are gold. He's about as close to perfect as a snowboarder comes.

At 10 years old, Tanner Hall first got into the sport of freestyle skiing, which was fortuitous considering how much success he would see freeskiing later in his life. From 2001 to 2008 Hall failed to win a gold medal at the X Games only once, and even in that lone year without top honors (2005), he still took home two silver medals. Ligament tears in both knees in 2009 effectively ended his X Games career but not before he laid down his roots as the most respected freestyle skier of his generation.

One of those rare athletes who has experienced elite success both at the Winter X Games and the Winter Olympics, Kelly Clark is a women's snowboarding legend who has dominated her sport for well over a decade and shows no signs of slowing down. Clark has medaled in three Olympics, including a gold medal in 2002, and also has 10 medals at various X Games events between 2006 and 2014. She is so respected in her sport that ESPN awarded her the Best Female Action Sports Athlete ESPY award in 2015, and she has every intention of competing at the 2018 Winter Olympics in Pyeongchang, South Korea.

When Sarah Burke got her start as a freeskier, there were no women's divisions or women's events, meaning she had to hold her own from the get-go against tough male talent. She did just fine in what once was a man's world and helped pave the way both for women in action sports and the superpipe event in freestyle skiing. In fact, she won five gold medals in that very event between 2007 and 2011 and almost certainly would have won more had she not passed away in a training accident in 2012. Sometimes the greats don't get long to stay that way, but Burke's success as a pioneer for women freeskiers is a legacy that lives on even after her death.

Career Snapshots

Skateboarding

MARK GONZALES 1984-1981

Transworld Skateboarding
Legend Award winner 2006

RODNEY MULLEN 1979-1990

Transworld Skater of the Year 2002
Inducted to Skateboarding Hall of
 Fame in 2013

TONY HAWK 1982-1999

12 NSA World Championships
10 X Games Gold Medals
62 contest wins

DANNY WAY 1984-2009

2-time Thrasher Magazine Skater
 of the Year
World record holder for Highest Air
 on a skateboard (25.5')
5 X Games Gold Medals

BOB BURNQUIST 1992- Present

12 X Games Gold Medals
7 X Games Silver medals
8 X Games Bronze medals

BMX

MAT HOFFMAN 1987–2003

2 X Games Gold Medals
10 World BMX Vert Championship
  Gold Medals
2005 Best Male Action Sports
  Athlete ESPY winner

DAVE MIRRA 1991–2013

14 X Games Gold Medals
6 X Games Silver medals
4 X Games Bronze medals

JAMIE BESTWICK 1996– Present

13 X Games Gold Medals
2 X Games Silver Medals
3-time Laureus World Sports Action
  Sportsperson of the Year

GARRET REYNOLDS 2002– Present

7 X Games Gold Medals
6-time NORA Cup Street Rider of
  the Year
2 Major all-around titles

NINA BUITRAGO 2005– Present

2010 world champion, Girls street,
  Cologne, GER
1st place, 2013 FISE World Series,
  Girls park, Montpellier, FRA

Career Snapshots

Motocross

BOB HANNAH 1974-1989

7 AMA National Championships
70 AMA National wins
Inducted to the AMA Motorcycle
   Hall of Fame in 1999

JEREMY MCGRATH 1986-2006

8 AMA National Championships
89 AMA National wins
Inducted to the AMA Motorcycle
   Hall of Fame in 2003

RICKY CARMICHAEL 1996-2007

15 AMA National Championships
150 AMA National wins
Inducted to the AMA Motorcycle
   Hall of Fame in 2013

TRAVIS PASTRANA 2000-2011

11 X Games Gold Medals
2 AMA National Championships
4-time Rally America champion

VICKI GOLDEN 2009- Present

3 X Games Gold Medals
2015 - Only woman ever to qualify
   for an SX Main Event race
2013 X Games bronze medalist

Extreme Winter Sports

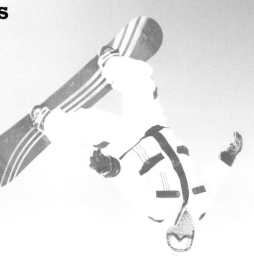

SHAUN PALMER 1983-2010

6 X Games Gold Medals
1 World Championship Gold Medal
1 Gravity Games Gold Medal

SARAH BURKE 1997-2012

5 X Games Gold Medals
1 World Championship Gold Medal
2007 Best Female Action Sports
   Athlete ESPY winner

TANNER HALL 1999-2013

7 X Games Gold Medals
4 X Games silver medals
30 competitive half-pipe and
   slopestyle victories

KELLY CLARK 1999- Present

1 Olympic Gold Medal
7 X Games Gold Medals
2008 TTR World Snowboard
   Champion

SHAUN WHITE 2000- Present

2 Olympic Gold Medals
13 X Games Gold Medals
2006 TTR World Snowboard
   Champion

A BASE jumper jumps from the KL Tower in Kuala Lumpur, Malaysia.

KL Tower

Words to Understand:

charismatic: having great charm or appeal

prodigies: young people who are unusually talented in some way

burgeoning: growing or developing quickly

CHAPTER

THE FUTURE OF EXTREME SPORTS

As far as competitive sports go, those events classified under the banner of extreme sports or action sports are relatively young. The first X Games were in 1995, while the NBA is pushing 60 years old, the NHL is just shy of its 100th birthday, and baseball's National League was founded all the way back in 1876. Just like those other sports have survived growing pains en route to overwhelming popularity, so too will motocross, skateboarding, BMXing, snowboarding, and every other extreme sport in due time.

THE POPULAR KIDS

The most intriguing potential future for action sports is for them to gain the respect of more traditional athletic platforms, most notably the Olympics. Shaun White, for example, arguably the biggest star in extreme sports, has in many ways become a household name because he won gold medals in halfpipe in both the 2006 and 2010 Winter Olympic Games. Competing in the Olympics gives extreme athletes more exposure and more respect from those claiming that action sports are not "real" sports, and as they gain in popularity, more events may be elevated to Olympic inclusion.

Today, the athletes themselves could not care less how the world views them, but there is no denying the appeal they have to a certain demographic of consumer. **Charismatic** nonconformists always will hold a special place in the hearts of younger fans, but these iconoclast athletes are starting to find a large stage on which to hone their craft and earn endorsement checks. Mainstream popularity is a financial boon for these sports' biggest stars, and it looks as if that mainstreaming has only just begun.

THE OLYMPICS

At the Sochi Winter Olympics in 2014, for example, slopestyle skiing debuted as an Olympic sport, with Winter X Games star Nick Goepper participating in both his traditional events and the new Olympic one only a week apart. It speaks volumes as to how much athletes like Goepper value the X Games when he would be willing to risk injury that close to the most time-honored athletic tradition in the history of humankind, but it also shows a shift toward extreme sports going mainstream, not that Tony Hawk and his video games didn't start that trend years and years ago.

Still, Olympic inclusion of extreme sports is a controversial subject among those athletes who actually participate in these sports because a huge part of the draw always has been the counterculture that surrounds so many of these activities, which typically do not employ anywhere near the amount of stringent rules an athlete must face in an Olympic setting.

Slopestyle skiing was added as a medal sport for the 2014 Olympic Games in Sochi, Russia.

Tough Mudder is a popular obstacle course run that has exposed hundreds of Americans to an extreme form of sport.

WEEKEND EXTREMISTS

So on the one hand, extreme sports seem to be trending toward becoming even more popular than they already are, but on the other hand, mainstream popularity potentially could damage part of what made the sports so attractive to so many young people in the first place.

Today, there are scores of Americans who have no idea they already have fallen in love with extreme sports, as hardcore mud runs like Tough Mudder, Spartan Race, and Warrior Dash currently draw in over 1.5 million participants a year. With a growing national emphasis on physical fitness and few more entertaining ways actually to get that exercise, exhausting obstacle courses that send runners on 3 to 6 miles (5–10 km) of filth-laden grief also continue to grow more popular. Even people who don't consider themselves extreme athletes love this sort of activity, and each year these mud runs grow increasingly prevalent.

Burnside Skatepark
Portland, Oregon

4 Seasons Skatepark
Milwaukee, WI

Woodside Motocross Track
Moray, Great Britain

Hawkstone Motocross
Shropshire, UK

Mammoth Mountain
Mammoth Lakes, CA

Crested Butte Mountain
Crested Butte, CO

FUTURE STARS

While there is some risk that purists always will prefer that these sports stay out of the spotlight, there still is little doubt that fans themselves will remain loyal to the stars they love, especially with so many promising young stars coming up to carry the torch that Hawk, White, Hoffman, and Mirra once lit.

Although it's hard to peg which of these young stars ultimately will find their way to X Games success and potential video game endorsements, there are a few young **prodigies** that are especially intriguing, most notably 11-year-old Japanese skateboarder Isamu Yamamoto, a YouTube star who has earned comparisons to skateboarding legend Rodney Mullen.

Tens of millions of people have watched Isamu's freestyle skateboarding videos online, proving his global popularity, although the fact that he is a Japanese athlete embracing a sport as American as skateboarding proves that one other way extreme sports could expand moving forward is through globalization. As more and more young people embrace action sports in countries all over the world, the possibility of them matching the more well-known sports in popularity increases.

Fans can keep up with the movements of their favorite connected stars like Isamu Yamamoto on Instagram and Twitter.

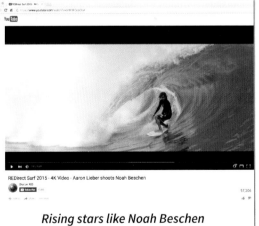

Rising stars like Noah Beschen use social media outlets like YouTube to build huge followings.

Other rising stars include teenage snowboarding prodigy Darren Mack, **burgeoning** surfing star Noah Beschen, and freestyle skiing standout Kelly Sildaru, but the beauty of today's plugged-in society means the next big thing in extreme sports could pop up on YouTube at any time. Thanks to the immediacy of social media, anybody could prove themselves worthy of rising to stardom in any extreme sport if they are to put in the hard work, and all it takes is one viral hit to turn a person into a legend.

Whether it be mainstream recognition in the Olympics, increased participation, and acceptance by schools and youth programs, or even just a boost in YouTube and social media views, it is impossible to ignore just how far extreme sports have come in so short a time and how high the ceiling appears for these activities moving forward.

Text-Dependent Questions:

1. At the Sochi Winter Olympics in 2014, which extreme sport made its debut?

2. Hard-core mud runs like Tough Mudder, Spartan Race, and Warrior Dash currently draw in how many participants a year?

3. Name the 11-year-old Japanese skateboarding prodigy who already has made a name for himself as a YouTube star.

Research Project:

Invent your own extreme sport for the next Olympics! Research manuals, tutorials, or videos for existing extreme sports, and then invent a new game. Draw diagrams or illustrations to help explain the rules. Share your work by publishing a rulebook for your sport.

GLOSSARY OF EXTREME SPORTS TERMS

adrenaline: a substance released in the body that increases the heart rate and provides more energy, usually during times of fear or excitement.

accolades: expressions of praise or marks of acknowledgement.

bungee jumping: jumping from a high place while attached to a long, stretchy rope that stops the jumper before hitting the ground.

contemporaries: people who are active during the same time period.

complacent: satisfied, not wanting to change.

credibility: able to be believed, accepted as truth.

criticism: comments made that disapprove of something or someone.

defunct: not in existence anymore.

dethroned: having taken the place of someone at the top of a sport or field.

dissuaded: convinced not to do something.

elements: the conditions a person is in, usually related to severe or extreme weather or environments.

exhibition: showing something in public, often referring to a surprising our outstanding performance, sometimes non-competitive.

fascination: having intense interest or feelings about something or someone.

gravitate: to tend to move toward something or someone.

halfpipe: a structure with high sides, made of metal or snow, used to do tricks using skateboards, snowboards, and so on.

influential: able to cause change or to inspire.

inherent: part of the nature of someone or something.

intoxicating: causing much stimulation, either emotionally or physically.

longevity: how long something lasts, for example, how long an athlete is able to participate in his or her sport.

mainstream: the current way something is done.

neurotransmitter: what carries messages from one nerve cell to another in the body.

parkour: a sport in which participants run, jump, or climb over obstacles as quickly as they can.

predecessor: someone who came before.

revolutionized: changed something completely.

showcase: to display or exhibit.

sponsorship: a deal in which an athlete is supported by a person or organization in return for advertising rights.

stamina: able to do something for a long time due to great physical or mental strength.

subjectively: judged based on perception, rather than objectively, usually relating to artistry, creativity, and style.

wakeboarding: riding behind a motorboat on a short board with foot straps and doing tricks while moving across the boat's wake.

CHRONOLOGY

1959: The first skateboards are sold in stores for $9.95.

1965: The first snowboard is invented when Sherman Poppen nails two wooden skis together.

1965: Teams from the U.S., Mexico and Japan compete in the first National Skateboard Championships in Anaheim.

1970s: French mountain skiers Patrick Vallencourt and Sylvain Saudan use the term "extreme" to describe their conquest of Chamonix Couloirs. (The term "extreme sports" quickly came to be applied to most new and dangerous sports).

1973: Frank Nasworthy revolutionizes the sports when he adapts the Cadillac wheel for his board.

1973: BMX bikes go on the market.

1976: The first commercial skateboard park opens in Carlsbad, California.

1976: The first downhill BMX race is held in Marin County, California.

1978: The first BASE jump is performed.

1979: The first modern bungee jumps are made from the 250-foot Clifton Suspension Bridge in Bristol, England.

1979: Inline skate are invented.

1983: ESPN presents a seven-race series for BMX bikes with $45,000 and new cars as prizes.

1984: The first bike stunt contests are held in skateboard parks in California.

1992: Freestyle skiing is a medal sport at the Winter Olympics in Albertville.

1993: The first World Skysurfing Championships are held in Spain.

1995: The first X Games, held in Newport, Rhode Island, are broadcast on ESPN to a national television audience.

1997: The first winter X Games are held in Big Bear Lake, California.

1998: Snowboarding is a medal sport at the Winter Olympic Games in Nagano.

1999: Superstar Tony Hawk completes the first backside 900 in competition.

2008: BMX racing is a medal sport at the Summer Olympic Games in Beijing.

2014: Slopestyle events in both skiing and snowboarding debut at the Winter Olympic Games in Sochi.

Extreme Sports today: For the 2018 Winter Games in Pyeongchang, South Korea, the IOC replaces the parallel slalom snowboard event with big air snowboarding and freestyle skiing. In these events, athletes hurtle down a huge snowy ramp up to nine stories high and fly off the edge to perform a series of flips and twists.

FURTHER READING:

Hurley, Michael. *Board Sports (Extreme Sports).* Raintree, 2015

Li, WenFang. *Extreme Sports (Getting the Edge: Conditioning, Injuries, and Legal & Illicit Drugs).* Mason Crest, 2014

Killcoyne, Hope Lourie. *Extreme Sports and Their Greatest Competitors (Inside Sports).* Rosen Education Service, 2015

Kalman, Bobbie/ Crossingham, John. *Extreme Sports (Extreme Sports-No Limits!)* Crabtree Publishers, 2004

INTERNET RESOURCES:

ESPN X GAMES: http://xgames.espn.go.com/xgames/

Motorcross America: http://www.motorcyclemuseum.org/asp/museum/exhibits/mx/history.asp

Web MD: http://www.webmd.com/fitness-exercise/extreme-sports-whats-appeal

Bleacher Report: http://theboardr.com/post/Skateboarding_Accepted_Into_the_2016_Olympics

VIDEO CREDITS:

Tony Hawk Dials Up the First-Ever 900: (pg 8) https://www.youtube.com/watch?v=x3uJNssoaQg

Dave Mirra Lands a Double Backflip (2000) (pg 9) https://www.youtube.com/watch?v=2uDGu9-Y0VA

Bob Burnquist Flirts With Perfection (2001) (pg 10) https://www.youtube.com/watch?v=3BqjGTDfuaw

Brian Deegan Flips for FMX (2003) (pg 11) https://www.youtube.com/watch?v=9f5Xwk843Ys

Travis Pastrana Double Backflips His Way Into America's Heart (2006) (pg 12) https://www.youtube.com/watch?v=pLtRW_7_piY

Nyjah Huston Proves Age Is Nothing but a Number (2006) (pg 13) https://www.youtube.com/watch?v=Ocb0yQuEfsg

James Kingston Takes Parkour to New Heights (2013) (pg 14) https://www.youtube.com/watch?v=KSwBT6QRUjA

Danny MacAskill Rides the Ridge (201415) (pg 15) https://www.youtube.com/watch?v=cdO-hdTOX8c

Courageous kayaker in a vertical diving position down a waterfall, approximately 45 feet high.

QR CODES AND LINKS TO THIRD-PARTY CONTENT

You may gain access to certain third-party content ("Third-Party Sites") by scanning and using the QR Codes that appear in this publication (the "QR Codes"). We do not operate or control in any respect any information, products, or services on such Third-Party Sites linked to by us via the QR Codes included in this publication, and we assume no responsibility for any materials you may access using the QR Codes. Your use of the QR Codes may be subject to terms, limitations, or restrictions set forth in the applicable terms of use or otherwise established by the owners of the Third-Party Sites. Our linking to such Third-Party Sites via the QR Codes does not imply an endorsement or sponsorship of such Third-Party Sites, or the information, products, or services offered on or through the Third- Party Sites, nor does it imply an endorsement or sponsorship of this publication by the owners of such Third-Party Sites.

PICTURE CREDITS

INDEX

In this index, page numbers in **bold italics** font indicate photos or videos.

INDEX